GANGSTERS, BOOTLEGGERS, AND BANDITS

HEATHER E. SCHWARTZ

Lerner Publications Company • Minneapolis

To my parents, Anita and Bruce MacDonald —H.E.S.

Lerner Publications Company
A division of Lerner Publishing Group, Inc.
241 First Avenue North
Minneapolis, MN 55401 U.S.A.

Website address: www.lernerbooks.com

Library of Congress Cataloging-in-Publication Data

Schwartz, Heather E.
    Gangsters, bootleggers, and bandits / by Heather E. Schwartz.
        p.   cm. — (ShockZone™—villains)
    Includes index.
    ISBN 978-1-4677-0604-9 (lib. bdg. : alk. paper)
    1. Gangsters—United States—History—Juvenile literature. 2. Gangsters—United
States—Biography—Juvenile literature. I. Title.
    HV6785.S387 2013
    364.1092'273—dc23   201201824

Manufactured in the United States of America
1 – CG – 12/31/12

TABLE OF CONTENTS

Broken laws, broken skulls, bullet holes. During the 1900s, gangsters made **a nasty mark** on the United States. These crooks were organized. They often worked in—you guessed it—gangs. And they were complicated characters.

Gangsters worked hard to clean the streets of other bad guys. But they definitely didn't work to clear out crime. Many gangsters were loyal—so loyal that they followed their friends to the grave. Others turned on their friends to save their own skin.

All gangsters lived on the wrong side of the law. Their crimes included just about anything you can think of. Robbery? Check. Drug smuggling? Sure thing. And don't forget car theft, illegal gambling, murder, and more. Gangsters also tended to be good at what they did. So good that many of them got away with their crimes.

Who were these hardworking hoodlums? Read on to learn more about some of the United States' most famous gangsters.

From left to right: Mobsters Paul Ricca, Salvatore Agoglia, Lucky Luciano, Meyer Lansky, John Senna, and Harry Brown photographed in New York in 1932

AL CAPONE: CHICAGO'S SCARFACE

Illegal gambling, robbery, murder—you name the crime, and Al Capone probably took part in it. He got his start early, skipping out on seventh grade to join a gang. Later, as a young man, he got into the fight that left him with a scarred left cheek. Not that Al needed a pretty face to succeed at mob life. Besides, Scarface was a great nickname for a gangster.

By 1925 Al was the top guy in Chicago crime. At that time, alcoholic drinks were banned across the country. Al made a fortune from bootlegging. He and his crew sold alcohol in secret. It was violent business. Al had a talent for taking out rival gangsters. That's what happened at the St. Valentine's Day Massacre, on February 14, 1929. Al's men dressed as police officers and gunned down some of his competition inside a garage.

> **bootlegging** = the illegal smuggling and selling of alcohol

The bodies of gangsters lie on the floor after the deadly St. Valentine's Day shootings. Al Capone ordered the killings to cut down his competition.

Everyone knew what Al was up to, including the Federal Bureau of Investigation (FBI). Even so, he was a tough guy to bust. Al's violent crimes went unpunished. But in 1932, the U.S. Treasury Department finally put him in prison. How? Turns out Al had earned about $100 million from his operations. He was busted for not paying his taxes on the money.

Al wound up spending more than seven years behind bars. He served some of his time at the new prison on California's Alcatraz Island. After his release in 1939, Al was ill for years. In 1947 he died of a stroke and pneumonia, a free but powerless man.

LIFE ON THE ROCK

Between 1934 and 1963, the U.S. government operated a maximum-security prison on Alcatraz Island (below). Surrounded by water, Alcatraz was 1.5 miles (2.4 kilometers) away from the shores of San Francisco, California. That's a long swim. Some of the country's most dangerous gangsters were sent to the Rock to shrink their chances of escape.

LESTER GILLIS:
BABY-FACED GANGSTER

A baby! So sweet! Oh...wait...that's no baby. That's Lester Gillis, better known as Baby Face Nelson. Yikes!

Baby Face Nelson started his career as a gangster in the 1920s. He was barely a teenager. His talent? Stealing cars. When he grew up, he moved on to more vicious crimes—like murder. Lester was so cruel when he killed that even Al Capone couldn't handle working with him.

At the age of twenty-three, Lester started robbing banks with another famous criminal, John Dillinger. The two of them had escaped jail together. When Dillinger was killed by FBI agents, Baby Face Nelson became Public Enemy No. 1. That meant the FBI was on his trail in a big way.

The results of the hunt were deadly on both sides. First, Lester killed the three FBI agents who found him hiding and holding hostages. With the agents dead, Lester got away. He went on to rob a bank, where he also killed a group of police officers.

Lester's crime spree ended in 1934. A car chase and shootout with the FBI exploded in the Illinois town of Barrington. Baby Face managed to escape, but he didn't survive long. Legend has told that he breathed his last breath in his wife's arms. Sounds like an OK way to go. But Lester's end was less peaceful than that. The law discovered his naked body in a ditch one day after the shootout.

Police inspect the body of Baby Face Nelson. He was shot full of bullet holes in 1934.

BONNIE AND CLYDE:
GANGSTERS IN LOVE

Ever heard of Bonnie Parker or Clyde Champion Barrow? Maybe not. But the names Bonnie and Clyde probably ring a bell. This gangster couple skipped dating and went straight to killing, kidnapping, and robbery. Not exactly romantic—but hey, it added drama to their lives.

Before Bonnie and Clyde met in Texas, they were regular folks who happened to be bored and poor. The time was the early 1930s. The United States was suffering through the Great Depression (1929–1942). Many people were out of jobs. Honest work was hard to find. Bonnie worked a crummy job to support herself. Her husband, Roy, was stuck in jail. Clyde lived in a crowded back room behind a gas station along with his parents and siblings. Clyde was more than unhappy about the state of the country. He was in a murderous rage.

The pair met in 1930. Their time together was cut short by a prison sentence for Clyde. (By then he was already a pretty good thief.) When Bonnie visited him, she met Frank Turner. Frank was Clyde's cellmate. He had big plans cooked up for Bonnie. Could she pick up a gun at his parents' house and smuggle it into the jail?

Frank told Bonnie that he'd use the gun to escape with Clyde. Bonnie just couldn't say no.

Drought in many areas of the country (above) and the stock market crash of 1929 led to the Great Depression. Joblessness spiked and some people turned to crime to make a living.

Once Clyde Barrow escaped from prison, he figured he'd better stay away from home for a while. But robbing gas stations and stealing cars didn't exactly help him avoid the law. Soon Clyde was sent to jail again. This time, he was forced to serve hard labor.

Clyde suffered abuses while in prison. He wanted out. So he asked another prisoner to chop off two of his toes. Clyde's injury sped things along. He was out in a week.

Bonnie Parker and Clyde barrow play around for the camera between robberies.

Back with Bonnie, the romance heated up. So did the couple's anger. Sure, Clyde was a criminal. But his awful time in prison didn't seem fair.

The couple rounded up a gang and took off traveling. This was no honeymoon, though. Working with their gang, they stole cars and robbed banks. They kidnapped victims and even murdered a few.

Soon the law captured other members of the gang. But Bonnie and Clyde continued their crazy crime spree.

In 1934 a so-called friend gave them up. Henry Methvin told his father, Iverson, about his criminal acts. Iverson Methvin and some law officers set a trap to capture Bonnie and Clyde.

Bonnie and Clyde's car, pictured here, was covered with bullet holes after the couple's final gunfight.

Iverson parked his truck on the side of the road as if it were stalled. Bonnie and Clyde approached in a car. Little did they know police officers were hiding nearby. As Bonnie and Clyde slowed down to investigate, gunfire broke out. Their car was riddled with bullets— and the couple inside lost their lives.

GUNSLINGER WITH A HEART OF GOLD

Despite her criminal ways, Bonnie Parker has been described as beautiful, smart, and sensitive. She was gifted in school and became famous for the poetry she wrote while running from the law. Bonnie was wanted for killing at least thirteen people with Clyde. But some people believe she didn't actually commit any murders herself.

MEYER LANSKY:
THE MOB'S ACCOUNTANT

Majer Suchowljanskiy was born into a poor family in Russia. In 1911 his family moved to New York City. Majer took the name Meyer Lansky. Within a few years, he began gambling and stealing cars. During the 1920s, he moved on to bootlegging. By 1928 he and his buddy Bugsy Siegel had built up their own business. Meyer and Bugsy ran a group of murderers for hire. The press named it Murder, Inc.

During the 1930s, Meyer gained power as a crime boss. He forced lawful businesses to give him money. He opened illegal casinos from New York down to Florida. He dabbled in the drug trade. The secret to his success? A ruthless attitude. He did whatever it took to succeed in his line of work. Legend has it that Meyer even ordered his old pal Bugsy gunned down.

Four of the members of Lansky and Siegel's Murder, Inc., sit in court in 1941.

Meyer was a super-organized crook. He became known as the Mob's Accountant. He collected millions over his lifetime. He also helped to develop the National Crime Syndicate. This group linked mobsters throughout the United States.

The sly Meyer wasn't easy to pin down. But like Al Capone, he made a dumb mistake. Officials arrested him for not paying his taxes. He was tried and acquitted. By the time the trial ended, Meyer was in poor health. He still had his freedom when he died of lung cancer in 1983.

acquitted = found not guilty of a crime

Lansky is all smiles leaving a courtroom in 1958.

JOHN GOTTI: POWER-MAD MOBSTER

John Gotti is proof: gangsters didn't go away as the twentieth century went on. John ruled mob crime in New York City in the 1980s. He got his start at the age of twelve, working for a huge crime "family" called the Gambinos. He was only an errand boy. But he worked hard—at bullying, fighting, and stealing—and dropped out of school when he was sixteen. It was the perfect path for a criminal lifestyle.

In the 1960s, John got married and had children. He tried to quit crime for a little while. But he just couldn't give it up. He kept on scheming with the Gambinos. In 1968 he landed in jail for theft. When he got out five years later, he murdered the members of another gang in a revenge plot. Surprisingly, he only served four years for the crime.

Three members of the Gambino crime family, *(left to right)* "Big Paul" Castellano, Joseph Castellano, and Paul F. Castellano, were arrested in 1975. John Gotti was part of the Gambino family.

The Gambinos must have liked John's work. The second time he left prison, he got a promotion. In the late 1970s, he started to lead his own crew. But he wasn't satisfied. A few years later, he had a falling out with the Gambino boss. In 1985 the boss was gunned down—on John's orders. John Gotti became the family's new leader.

His reign of power didn't last long. In 1992 John was convicted of murder and other crimes. His son stepped up to the boss role. John died in a prison hospital in 2002.

John Gotti's son, John Gotti Jr., took over for the mob boss when his father went to prison.

STEPHANIE ST. CLAIR: HARLEM HOODLUM

Stephanie St. Clair ran Harlem's illegal gambling during the 1920s and the 1930s. Stephanie was known across this New York City neighborhood for her fierce temper. When other gang leaders challenged her control, she didn't step down. That held true even when the gangster was Dutch Schultz. Dutch was tough. But he didn't scare Stephanie. War broke out between the two sides in the 1930s.

More than forty people were murdered as a result of the fighting. Stephanie's side began to lose. She fought back even harder. She claimed the police were helping Schultz harass her. She took out

Dutch Shultz (*above*) was St. Clair's toughest competition in the illegal gambling rings of Harlem.

newspaper ads saying the cops were corrupt. It was true, and Stephanie knew it. She'd paid them to look the other way while she ran her illegal operations.

Stephanie's finger-pointing didn't go over with the cops. Soon Stephanie was arrested on trumped-up charges. She spent eight months locked up.

When she got out, she realized she had to give up. She let Dutch Schultz and other gangsters take over in Harlem. In 1935 Dutch was shot. As he lay in the hospital, Stephanie sent him a telegram. "As ye sow, so shall ye reap," it said. Meaning, he got what was coming to him. Dutch died not long afterward. But Stephanie's hands were clean when it came to this crime. She'd had nothing to do with it.

People walk the streets of Harlem in the 1930s.

VINCENT GIGANTE: CRIMINAL CON MAN

Vincent Louis Gigante became the leader of New York's Genovese mob family during the 1980s. By that time, he'd committed all sorts of crimes—bribery, smuggling, murder, you name it. Vincent was one of the craftiest gangsters in history. This guy did everything he could to avoid being sent to prison.

Here's one example of Vincent's craftiness. He forbade others in the family to use his name in conversation, since the law might be listening in. Even his nickname, Chin, was off-limits. Instead, other gang members called him C in sign language or pointed to their chins.

Vincent "Chin" Gigante, looking dazed and confused, is helped along by his son as they leave Gigante's house in 1997.

By the 1970s, Vincent was sure the law was on his tail. He spent decades acting in public as if he were mentally ill. He wore pajamas, slippers, and a robe all day. He wandered the streets of his New York City neighborhood mumbling to himself. He even behaved that way in court. He gathered a group of psychiatrists to argue that he was legally insane. This would mean he could get out of a criminal trial.

Vincent had confessed to many of his mob buddies that he was faking. They wound up spilling the beans. FBI agents also caught him going to mob meetings in nicer clothes and behaving normally. In 1990 he was arrested on charges including murder.

In 1996 a judge declared Vincent competent to stand trial. He was soon convicted of plotting murders and other crimes. He may have been tricky, but he couldn't avoid his punishment forever. He died in prison more than halfway through his twelve-year sentence.

competent = able to understand the difference between what's legal and what's not

CHARLES ARTHUR FLOYD: PRETTY TOUGH GUY

Charles Arthur "Pretty Boy" Floyd wasn't a bad guy
through and through. Sure, there's no denying he was an outlaw.
He served time in jail for robbing a store. He held up many banks
during the 1920s and the 1930s. Rumor has it he even killed a
man. But this gangster only turned to crime because he felt beaten
down by poverty. Steady jobs were in short supply in his home
state of Oklahoma.

While that's not a great excuse for breaking the law, Pretty Boy
Floyd tried to do good too. That murder he may have committed?
It was his way of taking justice into his own hands. He believed his
own father's murderer had been wrongly set free. The money

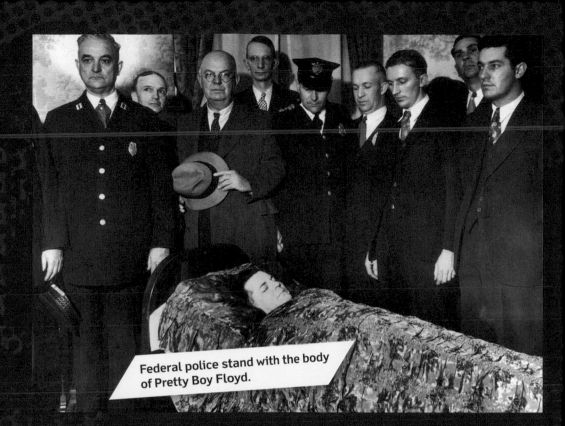

Federal police stand with the body of Pretty Boy Floyd.

he stole? He used some of it to buy food for hungry neighbors. And when Charles robbed banks, he destroyed mortgage papers. That way, people in debt would no longer have to pay for their land. Word got out and this gangster grew pretty popular.

Although the public thought of Pretty Boy Floyd as a hero, the FBI had another opinion. To them, he was Public Enemy No. 1 by 1934. When the law tracked him down, Charles got caught up in a gun battle. Gunfire struck him twice, killing him. Thousands of people attended his Oklahoma funeral. His life story was even made into a song by the famous folksinger Woody Guthrie.

Floyd inspired folksinger Woody Guthrie (above) to write the song "Pretty Boy Floyd."

SALVATORE LUCANIA: LUCKY LAWBREAKER

Salvatore Lucania didn't start out life so lucky. He and his parents moved to the United States from Italy in the early 1900s. Salvatore grew up poor on the streets of New York City. He soon joined a gang. By the age of ten, he was a hardened criminal.

Salvatore's luck began to turn. He won a lot of cash when he gambled. He avoided arrests. He even survived a murder attempt. He was beaten up, stabbed with an ice pick, and dumped on a beach. But *luckily,* he didn't die. Around the time of the attack, he began going by the name Lucky Luciano.

When Lucky took over as the boss of New York City's two biggest crime families, it wasn't by luck or by chance. He did what he had to do to gain control. That included murdering the families' former bosses.

In 1936 Lucky was finally sent to prison. His sentence was thirty to fifty years. But because he was so well-connected in the criminal world, the U.S. government asked for his help. It was another lucky break.

Lucky helped out in World War II (1939–1945) by organizing his criminal friends to catch German spies. His efforts paid off for the United States. They helped him personally too. Lucky was released from jail early. There was only one catch. He was deported back to Italy, where he died of a heart attack in 1962.

Lucky Luciano, arrested for drug trafficking, arrives at a New York courthouse in handcuffs.

deported = sent back to the country in which a person was born

JOSEPH BONANNO:
CRIMINAL CLIMBER

Joseph Bonanno came to New York from Italy illegally in 1924. First, he worked as a bootlegger. A little later, he started working for the mob boss Salvatore Maranzano. Maranzano was sort of a mobster mentor to Joseph. When Maranzano was murdered, guess who took his place? That's right: twenty-six-year-old Joseph Bonanno.

For years, Joseph dabbled in both legal and illegal activities. He put money into a dairy farm and a cheese company. He also created the double coffin, which allowed mobsters to hide one body underneath another before the burial. This was a cool trick, but not exactly a lawful one.

In 1964 Joseph disappeared from New York City. He reappeared two years later, claiming that rival mobsters had kidnapped him. But some people believed he was really just hiding out from his enemies. No one knows for sure, but this marked the beginning of the end of his life of crime. By 1968 he'd retired to Arizona. This was an unusual event. Most guys in his position weren't allowed to leave the business alive.

Reporters follow Joseph Bonanno through the streets of New York City in 1966.

Retirement wasn't relaxing for Joseph. His house was bombed. He had to go to court. And eventually, he had to serve some prison time for interfering with police work. But in 1983, he published a popular autobiography, *A Man of Honor.* Before he died, Joseph even got to see his life story played out on a TV miniseries.

GOING BANANAS

The New York press called Joseph Bonanno "Joe Bananas." He didn't appreciate the nickname. In the 1960s, Joe Bananas's mob family formed two rival groups. This became known as the Banana Split.

SAMMY GRAVANO: INFAMOUS FRENEMY

Sammy "The Bull" Gravano rose to power in New York's Gambino mob family. But that's not why he's famous. He's also the highest-ranking mob boss to turn on his friends. The Bull became a rat to save himself from serving a long prison sentence.

In the early 1990s, Sammy decided it'd be wise to talk to the government. It was time for him to make some confessions. He admitted he'd murdered nineteen people. He also ratted out thirty-six of his former mob pals, including John Gotti.

Sammy's old gang was out to get him. But the government rewarded Sammy for turning on his friends. For his crimes, Sammy got a light sentence of only five years. Then he disappeared into the safety of the Witness Protection Program. The program hides people who have spoken out about illegal activity. For a time, Sammy went by the name Jimmy Moran and ran a construction company in Arizona. He left the Witness Protection Program in 1997 to promote a book about his life.

Book tours and construction weren't all he was up to. He was also committed to committing more crimes. Where is he now? Where he belonged in the first place: serving twenty years in prison. He was caught dealing drugs in 2000.

In 1993 Gravano testified for the government in a case about corruption in professional boxing. Afterward, Gravano had to seek protection from his mob buddies.

FURTHER INFORMATION

Anderson, Dale. *The FBI and Organized Crime.* Broomall, PA: Mason Crest Publishers, 2010. Check out this book to discover how the FBI catches gangsters and other criminals.

FBI Kids Page
http://www.fbi.gov/fun-games/kids/kids
Visit this site to learn about how the FBI investigates criminal activity.

Horn, Geoffrey M. *FBI Agent.* Pleasantville, NY: Gareth Stevens Publishing, 2009.
Think you'd like to be an FBI agent? This book offers details about the job.

Matthews, Rupert. *You Wouldn't Want to Be a Chicago Gangster!* New York: Franklin Watts, 2010.
Get the scoop on the dangerous gangs that ruled Chicago in 1925.

The Mob Museum—National Museum of Organized Crime and Law Enforcement
http://themobmuseum.org
Planning a family vacation? The Mob Museum in Las Vegas, Nevada, gives visitors a real-life look at organized crime.

PBS Kids Go!—Big Apple History: The Crash
http://pbskids.org/bigapplehistory/business/topic19.html
The Great Depression set many gangsters on their criminal paths. Learn more at this site about a difficult period of American history.

Sloate, Susan. *The Secrets of Alcatraz.* New York: Sterling Publishing, 2008.
Read up on the history of this famous island that's gone from a prison to a national park

LERNER

SOURCE™

Expand learning beyond the printed book. Download free, complementary educational resources for this book from our website, www.lerneresource.com.

Main body text set in Calvert MT Std Regular 11/16.
Typeface provided by Monotype Typography.